Still, I Rise

A Soulful Tribute to Self

Vaishnnavi S

BookLeaf Publishing
India | USA | UK

Made with ❤ on the BookLeaf Publishing Platform
www.bookleafpub.in
www.bookleafpub.com

Dedication

I dedicate this book to my partner Abhi, who has always been there for me with kindness and support. To my kids, Ammu and Appu, for their endless love and the joy they bring. And to Auro, our golden—not just in breed, but in spirit—for his healing presence and love without judgment.

Love you all....

Preface

This book is a quiet unfolding—a collection of poems born from moments of stillness, struggle, healing, and hope. It is a journey inward, a gentle reminder that self-love is not a destination, but a daily practice of choosing yourself—again and again.

Each poem in these pages was written in conversation with the heart. Some came from wounds seeking light; others from joy rediscovered in unexpected places. Together, they reflect the messiness and beauty of learning to embrace oneself fully, flaws and all.

This is not a guidebook, nor a solution—it is a mirror. I offer these words not as answers, but as companions for anyone learning to love themselves a little more each day. May these poems hold space for your own journey, wherever you are on the path.

With tenderness,

V

Acknowledgements

This book would not have been possible without the love, patience, and presence of those who walked beside me—silently or with words, near or far—through the many seasons that shaped these poems.

To my parents—thank you for the roots that run deep, for the values you instilled in me, and for loving me in all my becoming. Your strength and grace are in every line I write.

To my partner, Abhi—thank you for being my steady ground, my calm in the chaos, and my greatest encourager. Your belief in me, especially on the days I doubted myself, gave these words room to breathe.

To my children, Ammu and Appu—you are my heart walking outside of me. Your pure love reminds me daily of what it means to be whole.

To Auro, our golden soul in fur—thank you for your quiet wisdom, healing energy, and unconditional love that never asked for anything in return.

To my siblings—thank you for being my first friends, my

mirrors, my anchors. You've taught me about love in all its beautiful, complicated forms.

To the friends who held space for my voice, even when it shook—thank you for reminding me that vulnerability is strength.

And finally, to the version of myself that chose healing over hiding, and softness over silence—thank you for showing up, for staying, and for daring to love again.

This book is for all of you.
With all my heart...
Vc..

1. The Self That Was, The Love That Is

A heart was held, though not always by gentle hands,
Yet still it beat—quietly, bravely—through the storm.
A soul was shaped by echoes of choices made,
By moments endured, and lessons worn.

Love had wandered, placed in others first,
But was never lost—only waiting, quietly near.
And now, the light within has softly grown,
Nurtured by time, no longer dimmed by fear.

The old self was honored, not forgotten,
For from its cracks, strength had bloomed.
Gratitude is whispered to every scar,
For they tell of battles passed, and rooms once gloomed.

No shame in choosing peace over pleasing,
No guilt in placing self above the rest.
The path was never perfect, only lived—
And in that living, love has found its nest.

Now, the self is chosen, again and again,
Not in pride, but in quiet knowing.
Love is given, but never at the cost
Of the garden within, always growing.

2. The Pause Between

Why was sadness worn like second skin?
Why was judgment allowed to echo within?
Why were their voices given such weight,
When the truth was never theirs to create?

Why was self-worth so easily shaken,
By glances given and words unspoken?
Why did seriousness wrap around the soul,
When lightness was always part of the whole?

A pause was taken, not in weakness, but in strength,
To breathe—to stretch thought at its length.
And there, in the silence, questions were laid bare:
Do their thoughts define what's truly there?

People judged. They always did.
But did it change the life quietly lived?
Did it alter the love that patiently grew,
Or rewrite the worth that always was true?

It didn't.
And it won't.

So the pause became peace.
The questions became truth.
And the weight... was finally released.

3. The Weight That Stayed

Rejection wasn't loud—it was quiet.
A silence that crept in after unanswered messages,
after doors that didn't open,
after trying to show up and still feeling invisible.

Loneliness didn't ask permission.
It just moved in—slowly—
between conversations that felt empty
and smiles that didn't quite reach the eyes.

Some days, the overwhelm came like a wave—
no warning, no space to breathe.
Everything felt like too much,
and yet, nothing could be dropped.

Tired wasn't just physical.
It was the kind of tired that sleep doesn't fix.
Tired of over-explaining,
of being misread, misheard, misunderstood.

Judged before being known.
Expected to shrink to fit someone else's comfort.
Every word weighed. Every silence questioned.

It wasn't dramatic.
It was just real.
Just... heavy.

But through it all,
even when the heart was stretched thin
and the mind was fogged over—

you kept going.
Maybe quietly. Maybe broken.
But still—
you.

4. This Is Not Sustainable

You need to stop—
not forever, just for now.
Stop sprinting through your own life
as if peace is a reward, not a right.

The chores will still be there.
The to-do list won't mourn
if a few boxes stay unchecked.

The dishes can wait in the sink.
The laundry doesn't mind the pile.
That file at work? It matters,
but not more than the body that carries you.

Time won't stop.
But that doesn't mean you have to race it.
You're not a machine—
you were never meant to be one.

This isn't living.

It's surviving on empty.
And you know deep down,
this isn't sustainable.

So breathe.
Let the mess sit.
Let the inbox wait.

You were not born
to be consumed by the day.
You were meant to live it.

5. Let It Begin With You

Be gentle with yourself.
Not just on the hard days,
but every day—
in the quiet moments,
in the rushed ones too.

Show yourself the love
you've been hoping to find in others.
Let your own arms be the first to hold you
when the world feels distant.

You give so much care—
to everyone else,
so freely, so fully.
Give some of that to you.
You deserve your own tenderness.

Stop looking for mirrors
in people who were never meant to reflect you.
Validation doesn't live out there.

It's built slowly, inside—
through truth, not applause.

Yes, the world will always have something to say.
You can't stop it.
You can't control it.
And you shouldn't let it anchor you.

Because if every step is weighed by their words,
your journey is no longer your own.
Their noise becomes your detour.
Their judgment becomes your delay.

So ask yourself—
Why does it matter?
Does it deserve that much space in your mind?
Is it needed?

No.

What's needed is this:
Grace.
Love.
Presence.
And permission—to be exactly who you are,
without explanation.

6. The Quiet Realization

In the search for echoes in distant places,
the heart is often left unheard.
Validation is gathered like scattered petals,
while the soul remains unstirred.

The one who breathes through each decision,
who stands within each storm,
is quietly forgotten
as the need to be seen takes form.

Moments are lived,
choices are made,
feelings are carried—
all by one constant presence...
You.

Yet rarely is that presence asked,
"What do you need to feel whole?"
For pleasing the world becomes the task,
while the self fades from the role.

And still,
within this very breath,
a truth begins to bloom—
Happiness is not found in mirrors,
but in the warmth of your own room.

Your worth is not a borrowed phrase,
not a nod, a like, a cheer.
It is the stillness in your chest,
the voice only you can hear.

So let this moment be the turning—
a gentle, quiet start.
Validation, softly blooming,
from the garden of your heart.

No power shall be given away,
no voice shall rise above.
For the one who matters most
is held in your own love.

7. Thankful

Thankful...
For the hurt,
For the pain,
For the heartache that cracked me open.

Thankful for the rejection,
The silence,
The spaces where love never showed up.
For the numbness that followed—
A teacher in disguise.

Thankful for the wounds,
For the tears that carved rivers through the nights,
For the loneliness
That taught me how to sit with myself
And listen.

Thankful for the lessons—
Some understood,
Some still unfolding in their own time.

Thankful for every experience,
Every moment,
Every decision.
Some were golden,
Some were messy,
Some—downright awful.
But all of them?
Essential.

Because without them,
I wouldn't be me.
I wouldn't be here.

And I wouldn't trade a thing.

Grateful...
For the path that shaped me,
For the becoming that still continues.

I love her—
The girl I was,
The woman I am,
And the soul I'm still growing into.

All her versions.

All her shades.
All her strength.

8. Gratitude in Every Scar

The hurt was welcomed as a teacher,
The pain was held in gentle hands,
The heartache was felt and released
In quiet, healing lands.

Rejection was granted as guidance,
Avoidance was offered like a sign,
Numbness was woven into armor,
Softly forging strength of mine.

Wounds were bestowed in hidden hours,
Tears were shed to cleanse the soul,
Loneliness was embraced in shadows,
Lessons carved, making me whole.

Each moment was given—bright or bleak,
Each decision placed with care;
Some were joyous, some were bitter,
Yet all shaped the path I bear.

And nothing is wished to be altered,
For all was needed to set me free;
The self was built in every version—
Past, present, future—lovingly.

Now I stand in quiet gratitude
For every chapter, dark or bright,
And in this gentle, whispered thanks,
My becoming is bathed in light.

9. The Unseen Weight

When it's you...
Mistakes are magnified,
Pointed at with sharp fingers,
Labeled as your fault—
Because you're home,
Because you should have known,
Because... it's your role.

But when it's them?
It's just a bad day.
An oversight.
Not a big deal.
Let it go.

You follow the rules,
Live inside invisible boundaries,
Carry silent expectations—
Because you have the time,
Because you don't have another job,
Because you're just... here.

Groceries.
Meals.
Kids.
Their diet, their meds, their moods—
Their tantrums, their tears,
Their disrespect that cuts like glass.
You tend to all of it.
Quietly.

And still...
You're the one falling behind.
The one too tired.
Too emotional.
Too much—
Or not enough.

While they—
Smile sweet to the world,
Wear charm like a mask,
Get praised for crumbs,
And escape the weight
They expect you to bear whole.

Yet, you're blamed.
Again.
And again.

This...
They say,
Is the feminine role.
The quiet sacrifice.
The strength that's never thanked.
The love that bends and breaks
But never leaves.

But hear this:
You are not weak for feeling this.
You are not wrong for wanting more.
You are not lesser because you're tired.

You are human.
And you deserve softness,
Support,
Respect.
Not just survival.

10. The Silence Between Us

She is silent,
not because she has nothing to say,
but because every word risks a wound
she's not ready to feel again.

He is distant,
not because he doesn't care,
but because opening his heart
might let the pain rush in.

They sit in the space between longing and fear,
where glances replace confessions,
and love—once loud—
fades into a quiet ache.

With each moment unspoken,
each touch withheld,
the fire dims,
and the distance grows colder.

Until one day,
they both look back—
and realize the love they once held
is now just silence
echoing through empty hearts.

They loved me when I dared not hope,
When I believed the bar too high—
Yet fate conspired in secret ways,
And brought their love to light.

Once found, it never fades,
Though distance stretches far and wide;
Our hearts, like lock and key,
Fit perfectly side by side.

We cheer each other on,
Celebrate each victory,
Offer shoulders in the storm,
And share our history.

This bond defies all words,
This love knows no boundary;
With acceptance, trust, respect—
Together, we are free.

11. Onwards and Upwards – A Second Sunrise

I've seen the storm, I've felt the fall,
Faced the silence, braved it all.
No more dreams on shaky ground,
No more waiting to be found.

Expectations laid to rest,
No more ache within my chest.
The hurt has taught, the scars have sealed,
A heart once torn—now gently healed.

Nothing shocks, no tear repeats,
I've danced through fire, stood through defeat.
It's time to turn, to face the light,
To step ahead with quiet might.

New memories wait down winding roads,
Where hope returns in lighter loads.
A second chance, a spark, a flame—
This time, I rise and play the game.

So go, and get it—claim your sky,
Don't ask for wings—just learn to fly.
The past is done, the page is clear,
Onwards now—your time is here.

12. She Rose in Fire, She Blooms in Gold

From silent ash, her soul took flight,
A whisper blooming into light.
The flames once cruel, now gently guide,
A journey born from pain and pride.

Her shattered heart, once torn apart,
Was mended slow, with sacred art.
Each crack a mark of where she grew,
Each scar a place the light shines through.

She rose not just to simply live,
But to reclaim, to heal, forgive.
A Phoenix wrapped in petals bold—
With roots in ash, and wings of gold.

She blooms again, not as before—
But deeper, wiser, something more.
For in the fire, she found her name,
And in the bloom, she stoked her flame.

13. Dare to Live Loudly Again

Dare...
To fall in love once more,
To open doors you closed before.
To give your heart, unchained, unguarded–
To feel it race, though once it parted.

Let someone feel they're truly seen,
And know what being special means.
To hold and heal, to laugh, to try–
To reach for stars across the sky.

Get up.
Show up.
Get decked in fire and flair.
Let your glow catch every stare.

Watch the eyes, the heads that turn,
Feel that old familiar burn.

The beauty bold, the beast within—
Both ready now to rise again.

Bring back the retro, raw, and wild,
The messy, fearless, freeborn child.
Live it loud, without regret—
The best days haven't happened yet.

Because life...
It only comes around this way once—
So dare to dance, to dream, to love,
To take the second chance.

14. Love Finds You in the Chaos

In the heart of chaos,
love gently finds you—
a silent whisper from the universe,
reminding you softly
that this isn't your ending.

This storm won't last forever,
your story doesn't end here.
This is not your final page—
just the closing of one chapter,
and the quiet awakening
of something beautifully new.

15. Letting Go with Grace

Some things can't be fixed once they're broken.
They could've been mended when the first crack showed
—
when the silence was still tender,
and the distance could still be crossed.

But now, it's shattered.
Not every piece remembers where it belonged.
And that's okay.
Let it rest, gently. Let it rest with grace.

Yes, it hurts—for both.
But even love stories, written with care,
sometimes need a quiet, necessary ending.

It's not a test of how much pain you can endure,
or a race to prove how hard you tried.

You can choose to bow out with dignity,
to honor what was once sacred,

and to let go—
not in defeat,
but in reverence.

16. Shift the Small, See the Big

You won't make a difference
by doing the same old thing every single day—
hoping for a spark,
yet lighting no new flame.

The outcome never shifts
if the input stays unchanged.
When life feels stuck,
when plans don't flow your way,
it's not always the world...
sometimes, it's your rhythm that needs a tune.

Maybe it's your routine,
your mindset,
your morning start,
or the story you repeat in your head.

Even the tiniest shift—
a new habit,

a kinder thought,
a deeper breath—
can ripple out in ways you never imagined.

You don't control everything—
that's where grace, fate, and the universe step in.
But what you do control—
your effort, your choices, your reaction—
that's where the magic begins.

Make your difference there.
And you'll find, one change at a time,
regret never gets a place to stay.

17. Find Yourself Before You Find Your Soulmate

In the journey to find your soulmate,
don't forget to find you first.
Embrace the mess and the magic—
the you that was,
the you that is,
the parts that broke,
and the strength that rose.

Love yourself without conditions.
Compliment your own soul.
Do the things that light you up.
Choose the love you wish to feel—
and give it to yourself, fully.

Because when you meet your soulmate,
they won't be completing you—
they'll be celebrating the wholeness
you already own.

And maybe, just maybe,
you'll be the spark
that sets their soul free too.

But always remember—
you can't pour love from an empty cup.
So fill yours first,
with grace, with joy,
with unapologetic self-love.

18. Love Them, But Love Yourself a Little more

How easy it is to lose yourself
for the ones you love...
To shrink your needs,
silence your voice,
and carry the weight
they never asked you to bear—
nor noticed you did.

You bottle up your feelings,
hide your pain behind smiles,
hoping one day they'll see,
they'll understand,
they'll love you back
the way you love them.

But time passes...
And slowly,
the cheerful you fades.
The dreams you once held close

gather dust.
Joy becomes unfamiliar.
Even the things that once lit you up
start to feel too far away.

And in that ache,
you begin to seek love
in the eyes that never truly looked.
You crave validation
from hearts that only took.

Because sometimes,
love isn't mutual—
It's mutually exclusive.
You give, they receive.
You bend, they stand.

But listen—
Keep loving them if you must...
just love yourself a little more.

Be proud of your tiny wins.
Admire your softness,
your strength,
your tired eyes,
your brave heart,
your scars that tell stories.

Even the broken nail,
the silver strands of wisdom,
the silence you turned into survival.

That's your magic.
And the universe...
it's listening.

So stop grieving the version of you
that sacrificed everything—
and start living
for the one who's still here...
you.

19. When Love Feels Like Home

Life becomes beautifully simple
when someone believes in your dreams
more fiercely than you do yourself.

And when that someone is your better half,
your best friend, your soulmate—
life doesn't just feel complete,
it feels like home.

With them, you're seen without masks,
heard without speaking,
loved without conditions.
You laugh louder, cry softer,
heal quicker, and live deeper.

Their criticism may sting,
but it's the mirror you need—
honest, raw, and rooted in love.
They won't always say "I love you,"

but they'll brew your morning tea,
push you to drink water,
remind you to sleep,
to move, to pause, to breathe.

They'll surprise you with quiet kindness—
a gift you whispered months ago,
a class you always wanted to take,
space when you need it most,
and pride in your every win,
without needing the spotlight.

A soulmate like that—
they don't rescue you from storms,
they walk beside you through them,
hand in hand,
heart with heart.

It's in the stolen kiss during morning chaos,
the shared silence that speaks louder than words,
the way they remind you, every day,
that you belong.
Completely. Truly. Rightfully.

Love like this isn't loud—
it's steady. It's sacred.
It's the kind that builds dreams,

braves battles,
and makes even the hardest life
feel soft and beautiful.

To live with your right one—
your soulmate, your best half—
is to live a life
where every ordinary day
feels nothing short of extraordinary.

20. Let the Little Things Go Wrong… So the Big Things Can Go Right

If you aren't willing
to let a few small things slip,
to face a little discomfort,
a bit of chaos,
a moment of uncertainty—

You might never open the door
to the extraordinary.

Growth demands risk.
Dreams ask for courage.
And the big wins in life
rarely come wrapped in perfect plans.

Sometimes, the cracks in the routine
are where the light gets in.

So take that step.
Let the little things wobble.
Because what's waiting for you
is far bigger than what you fear losing.

21. Honor Her Journey

You have grown.
You have learned.
You've come so far.

Be proud–
of this new version of you,
the one who handled storms
she never imagined she could.

Of the wars she fought and hid,
the ones no one knows,
the ones she quietly lost,
and the ones she bravely won.

Of the brave face she wears,
the way she still shows up–
every single time.

Applaud her.
Become her, more and more.

Love her.
Give to her.
Stand by her.

Respect her journey—
for it was never easy,
but she made it beautiful.